A Confusion of Marys

Rupert M Loydell

Sarah Cave

A Confusion
of Marys

Shearsman Books

First published in the United Kingdom in 2020 by
Shearsman Books Ltd
PO Box 4239
Swindon
SN3 9FN

Shearsman Books Ltd Registered Office
30–31 St. James Place, Mangotsfield, Bristol BS16 9JB
(this address not for correspondence)

www.shearsman.com

ISBN 978-1-84861-696-7

Some of these poems were previously published in
Amethyst Review, *Christianity & Literature*, *I Am Not A Silent Poet*, *New Writing*,
The Quint: an interdisciplinary journal from the north, *Stride*.

CONTENTS

'The opposite of faith is not doubt, but certainty. Certainty is missing the point entirely. Faith includes noticing the mess, the emptiness and discomfort, and letting it be there until some light returns.'
  —Anne Lamott, *Plan B: Further Thoughts on Faith*

'If one can remember a thing
One never experienced,
Think how easy the forgetting.'
    —Eric Pankey, 'The Dictates of Gravity'

'Every single song is one shadow of the whole.'
    —David Rothenberg, *Sudden Music*

Annunciations

ANNUNCIATIONS

Crooked crosses and all sorts of heavenly light: blue rain, reflections in skyscraper glass, firestorms, neon, a distant sun, a sculpted moon beneath an empty hanging robe.

Mary finds herself alarmed and shocked, intruded upon, over and over again. Heavenly creatures appear in her apartment, lean in through the window, recline next to her on the beach, or turn up when she's shopping, trying to have time alone. They all say the same impossible thing.

Who knows how this might work out? How the idea will be sustained, the miraculous remembered, in the future?

•

She cannot escape the idea that she is special, but she is not ready for this. Alone in the bus shelter, she tries to summon the courage to keep her appointment for a termination, as the advertising angel peers down from the hoarding at the other end of the bench, trying to sell her toothpaste. It is, she knows, her right to choose, and she will not heed the prophets, friends or soothsayers who say otherwise, or those who predict that this simple operation might skew, or end, her world.

•

She wakes to the sound of trumpets, to curtains fluttering in the city breeze. Her cat is already crying for food, ignoring the angelic apparition floating above her, slender trumpet in hand.

He finishes his sprightly tune, coughs, then starts to speak. She cuts him short. 'I'll call the cops,' she says.

He wobbles slightly in the air. 'You wouldn't?' he smiles. 'After all the practicing I've done?'

11

'For what?' she says.

'You've been chosen,' he says. 'You're special. Though only God knows why.'

'Special? Sure!'

'No, you are. You're going to have his child. I've come to tell you.'

'Yeah, of course I am. My boyfriend left me months ago. You didn't did you?' She smooths her nightgown.

'No, I didn't. Angels don't. We're holy servants, nothing more. Messengers and announcers, musicians and choristers too.'

'Well, go sing your song elsewhere. I've got to go to work. And take your trumpet with you.'

He's gone. There are car horns and shouts outside, and she can hear the owner of the café across the street unlocking his door and opening up. If she skips a shower she can get a bagel and an espresso before she has to leave. Might soothe her nerves and wake her up, sweep the jazz and bullshit from her mind.

•

Andy Warhol's annunciation is empty. Nobody says anything to anyone. A hand blesses the bottom left corner, a curtain is about to be pulled on the right. Trees and mountain point to heaven beyond a wall and a foregrounded tomb. The sky is flat, outline drawings are not aligned. The print is available in a variety of colours to suit the colour of your wall.

•

This one's a riotous swirl of action, with a frightened Mary at the centre of it all. An angel, wings erect and out of proportion, is telling her how it is and what will be, while animal-headed creatures watch on, having already destroyed her house. At the mercy of the elements, bathed in both celestial and moon light, she is caught in an awkward pose, afraid and shocked, surprised. Heaven and hell compete to draw a circumference around her and take the proffered lily for themselves. This ring of chaos is the moment a pebble gets dropped into the water and ripples slowly move away.

•

Why these empty arches, these porticoes full of light and air? What is a portico anyway, and why does she have to sit here quietly, pretending something is about to happen? Mary feels out of focus, blurred, as the world changes and shifts around her. She might turn to stone, or become dust. She doesn't like to ponder such things – look what happened last time.

There is always an interfering angel, who insists on speaking, however much she stops her ears or gestures from him to go away, even if she shouts or screams at him directly. Oh how she wishes he would leave and not tell her what she does not want to hear. She'd like to marry the carpenter and raise a couple of normal kids. A halo will simply get in the way, and she has never liked blue or the idea of crucifixion.

•

On the beach there are casts of angels, covered at high tide, proud and lifesize when the water's receded. You can wander among them and imagine them whispering to each other, telling you what will become of you, insisting it's for the best. You shake the sand from your shoes and think about an ice cream, walk along the promenade toward the distant pier. But the angels are patient and persistent, know you will meet again.

•

The angel's a shadow, a monoprint, a fashion model lounging on a rooftop shoot. He's gorgeous, he's naked, invisible, worried, concerned; a little bit creepy to tell the truth.

Strip away the feathers and you're left with only light or after-images of where they once were. You might have imagined it all, but something was there, you're sure.

The angels are shadows, squidges of ink, liars, imposters and frauds. They're enforcers of patriarchy, symbols of power, and they make you worried and concerned.

Strip away your self-confidence and all you're left with is a little girl, the memory of who you were. You might have grown up, have imagined it all, but *something* was there, you're quite sure.

•

The sea whispers to her, suggesting she will have a son, that he will change the world. The horizon holds steady but her heart is pounding and her eyes fuzzy with tears and disbelief, reflected light. She cannot focus on the waves, they won't stay still; she has not noticed that her shoes and feet are wet. Out of her depth and scared, she knows she cannot swim away from what she has just heard.

•

There is, says one art critic, an innate capacity for motherhood in all women, but each must find it for themselves. The new order is not always welcome, although paintings of Mary and the angel often evoke radiance and renewal. But there is terror and disruption, too, impossible distances crossed, as creation's extremes collide.

It is the beginning of a story that ends in suffering and death, it is a violation of a woman's body, it is the fulfilment of prophecy or the start of a great religion, depending on your point of view. All this triggered by an angel's sentence to a chosen girl, thrust into pregnancy and motherhood too soon.

•

Tear it up, tear it apart; the story survives. Re-imagined as a love affair, science fiction, or abstract colours in a square, it remains the story of a moment when something 'other' enters our world.

Of course, there were previous sightings, ecstatic visions or strange dreams, but this one seems the most well known, the one most explored in art. Symbolism thrives in contemporary and more traditional work: sacred blue, virginal white, empty chambers and porticos, lilies and descending doves, rays of light, winged angels and orderly gardens. We are reminded of the past, Adam and Eve exiled from Eden. Swirls of colour tell us the world will not last for ever.

Deconstructed or abandoned, forgotten or overlooked, the story always returns, gets told again. However much we disbelieve in angels they fly into our imagination and speak to us, tell us the same truths again, wings spread ready to catch the wind.

•

This angel's a bit of a budgie, pouting and preening in the mirror before he makes an entrance. All feathershake and swirling robes, he jumps in and proclaims in his most seductive tone. She doesn't seem to notice him, lowers her eyes to the floor and looks worried. He doesn't like being ignored, simpers and says his piece again. She doesn't move at all, but he knows she's heard his speech, decides it's time to go. She'll never know what a vision he is.

•

The scale of the human is out of all proportion to the angel. It's not that the latter is huge, he just fills the room with his presence, his light, and the words he speaks consume the previous silence. There's a hint of excess and adornment: the angel doesn't belong here but now he is everything is overshadowed and clearly illuminated. Colours flatten into bright tones, there are no dark corners any more, nothing is hidden except in Mary's heart. She wonders and ponders, consumes the moment before the room empties and the colours fade into centuries old frescoes in an empty church.

•

This angel is a snake, all sleek reptile print, crowd-surfing across the room to loud music. He spots a girl in blue and slides towards her, as the band allow a guitar solo to resume. He drops to the floor and writhes, turns to the girl and speaks.

It's not the chat-up line she was expecting, and she's never met anyone called Gabriel before. He dances with her for a while, then slithers back towards stage front, ready for the encore. She hangs back this time, watching and observing, listening as the song of praise and yearning swells.

•

He does a dance in front of her, embarrasses her on the street. He jumps, gyrates and escalates the moment into something else. She blushes, tries to escape; he's having none of it. He knows her name and where she lives, moves in circles around her. She relents and smiles, walks along beside him. He tells her when the baby's due; she knows he's not the father. The last she sees of him is summer's dust kicked up as he turns the corner.

•

Moon song, fixed smile of light, a slice of neon cheese. Representing distance, knowing, holiness; the universe without/within.

A drape of cloth, ill-fitting robe, a linen cascade above. Representing a stranger, flown in unannounced.

I marvel at the simple juxtaposition of two forms, made to share a space.

The Autophagy of Mary

As a cradle Christian / I can't help mediating
my impression of Mary through men / At the turn
of the century I sit down / to write
an idyllic longing for childhood / a re-writing
of all four gospels scored

into my confusion of Eden
a walled garden / guarded by the avenging

John Steed / his umbrella a sword
against the Nephilim / Sunday afternoons

are unaware of themselves / my niece spends her time
painting empty hen eggs / trying to remember
content / Firstly the Creed / these words

written by the early Church fathers / have become
more comprehensible over the years / If the Church mothers
had been present / their faces are now erased
and wait to be uncovered by revisionists

Re-vision / to alter something in the light of further evidence
Altar form
the light
    of something
that fades

with further
evidence

while all the official channels of faith are drawn
by men they are given by women / Women curate
the experience / women like my Grandmother
her Great Grandmother / who made the church
smell sweet on Sundays / giving lessons

on re-interpretation / whispering kindness

gender is an unnecessary addition to plant reproduction

                                    / Her flower arrangements
surround the choir and irritate the organist / A woman priest

though her words are simple and few

in Winchester Cathedral / reads a small sermon
from the pulpit / scenes of a violent nature
everyday liturgical events

'We are as stained glass to Christ's word'

goes her simile

Hebrew scripture
scratches out names
our fickle God is
autocannibalised
by the process

The toddling Ishmael
unsteady on his feet

Hagar the Egyptian
lights the pyre

wild raspberries in the desert
a bitter basket
a laughable sacrifice

goes her metaphor

The stern women in the church
who hand out the book of common prayer
relish the anachronistic language / remembering
the hothouses of their youths / The motherly
women who organise local community events
watch my niece / her two aunts / their matrilineal echo
in the eaves of the meeting house

as

she plays on the lawn

                                         and then there's my mother
firmly mine / in this rare moment of un-slippage

as

she sits in the pew / crumbling to something
beyond herself / a moment outside
of language / She introduced
me to the sacrament / and together
but always separate / we pray
at the many altars of her doubt

on her lips are prayers and Labour Party committee minutes

of obedience
of protest / her CND pin tabbed to my lapel

cast off the shadows of yesterday / shoulder to shoulder into the fray

1908 / 1936 / 1974 / 2001 / ?

My father / an atheist / was proud
to argue with the vicar / Now I think
about it / I can't remember once seeing
him in church / I suppose he went
there for my christening / My mother-in-law
tells me the story

of her son's christening / a private service
in the cathedral / an Anglican nun mentions our sins
in grey / how we hide our faith

in paper bags / concealing titles of religious novels
and forget the corporate body of Christ

I hide my paperback copy of *The Eagle and the Dove* in my coat pocket

Nevermind the silent and alone
saviour in the desert

dancing in the wind / says Bernadette

I learned the creed / alone
sat in the choir pews / maudlin

in the chapel at university / The creed embodied
a deep cut / a vertical line / a scar
in the ether / the one that the pulpit Shee La Na Gig
proudly shows to those who look up
beneath the clenched hands

of the priest / this design detail
as obscene and transcendent as so many
of my heretical beatitudes
unfolding through
life / My niece

our daughters' daughters will adore us / and they'll sing in grateful chorus

looks through a microscope at my
bug-like being / the viscose body
seeking solace / solitude / in the shade
of the grass / Veronica asks me why she
should accept that Aristotelian self-reflection
must rest like little flowers
in her hands when they bury her / why must
she wait / Her question starts a forest fire
Her question burns me / I have no answer

She buries my body in a cave / Her brothers Ishmael and Isaac
plant a garden / Years later they name it
the Cave of the Patriarchs

This morning / Father Matthew isn't concerned
about the number of pagans in the choir / Nine pagans
to four Christians and one non-committal / The four
Christians are all different denominations / Matthew isn't worried
about the irregularity of the sonnet / just happy to have
a full church and to know that choral music resonates
beyond the walls of the tribe /

                                    Music is God's weapon.

I first became aware of the Marian form
at my sister's first nativity / My sister
wore blue and cradled a swaddled Sally-doll

her hair chopped roughly / Four others
sitting beside her in white / sing
the pop song *Mary had a boy-child*

Women are the only exploited group
in history to have been idealized
into powerlessness. —Erica Jong

As a cradle second-wave Feminist / Mary's
mystical experience was whitewashed / Anger
at the male gaze prevented empathy

it took years for Mary to become / a defiant symbol
of how stoic women could be / My anger was as much Mary's
as it was my own / Women such
as my mother / grandmothers / great grandmothers
all silent in their marriages
the uphill struggle / the joy of the summit

the solitary contemplation of the mountain

                    / their imagined fortitude became

a banner / Mary's face
crumpled suffragist crinoline

I think of Eric Gill / the utopias he created
and how as a father figure he betrayed me

my father's memoirs of how
youthful he once was

from thence he shall come to judge the quick and the dead

His paternal betrayal written as grim realism / his sexual exploits
stone carvings / in my mother's stations of the cross

Poor Daisy Hawkins / she never knew
that she had been abused / as the grass rustled

and the saints pass this way / my sister and her
friends prune their leaves at the bathroom mirror
never knowing they had been abused

all things visible and invisible

Joseph / the exasperated male
Matthew / concerned to preserve the Cuckold's name
Paul / I'll never forgive

He who can't fit
the pre-conceived
ideal of gentlemanly masculinity

This man / a cut-up image
a surrealist dream of brown-paper
19th century classics versioning
a sticky-tape God / His eternal
absence / While walking

the dog one evening / these icons
of fearsome / replete femininity appear in the woods
as waxen figures in dissolution

At the altar / I stand with my mother and my mother-in-law
in the shadow of the cross

Wednesday's child

On Wednesday / I accidentally attend mass
at Westminster Cathedral / The church is full of devotion

Three women pray at the shrine of Mary
mother of God / clutching her feet
stroking her dress / I watch one woman
slip her hand lovingly between the statue's legs

The same day / Evensong at St Paul's is a tourist event
but silently I am dying with the Lord /

Music is our casement.

I stand with the Four Marys at the foot of the cross
our school uniforms crumpled / our early sexual experiences

are written in a code / we spend our twenties

translating

how little I knew / You
gave me these end of days as / An embrace

The men can't make it / But John / John is here
John is fluid like merging shadows / a transtemporal 'they'

The other Apostles disbelieve John's account.

Wednesday's child

Christ not only brought his mother
sorrow / also joy

'God has brought me laughter and everyone
who hears about this will laugh
with me.' – Sarah

Wednesday's child is full of woe

I have written about Mary as though she were exploited
by her encounter with the divine / perhaps she was
but then I would have to accept that God was gendered

White is
mother's submission / Black is His
fire a concession
Mary is matter / Christ is light

'Faith is all hot air!' says Mr Banks 'so let's go fly a kite!'

Mary submits to the news
with good grace / Joseph declares that 'all shall be well' and
they're not to worry about material possessions anymore
'The revolution has saved us!' / They cling to the furniture
while the cannons are still firing /

those who don't fit   their anger always righteous
                                        and unjust / A reaction to the burn

            Without submission
to male idealisation of weakness
how can Mary's mystical experience be reclaimed?

Must Gabriel appear in the male form?

'No' says Catholic.com / 'Angels are an altogether other
being / Not defined by gender / Not given in marriage.'

With the exception of the Nephilim / 'But of course
the bible contradicts itself'
murmurs my Grandmother / Veronica's
great Grandmother/ half-asleep on the sofa

Gabriel's masculinity defines the moment
culturally not spiritually / Mary's virginity is of no interest
until the male presence of the angel walks in
and takes control of her fate / Mary's small stature

emphasises the humbleness
of her situation and is in line
with mystic tradition / But if God is ungendered
and indeed 'un'-everything
then gender politics is irrelevant / Negative theology creates
an even playing field / Mary in her state of humble confusion
is human and now in the perfect state
in which to receive God / When God is present
She grows bigger with the knowledge
of things and finally
gives birth to God made flesh

'Is there some comparison to be made
between the birth of Christ
and the opening of the Ark of the Covenant
in the first Indiana Jones film' / I ask one morning
on the way to school / 'Certainly / the screams
might be resonant if not the melting faces'

'You should have been present at the birth of my first'
my mother answers

A metaphor for creation?

Mary needs no male mediation / turn her inside
out / She is still
the mediator of creation

The Ark of the Covenant

With modern fertility treatment at her disposal / Sarah
could have saved Hagar the strife

Ishmael would have remained under a bush
Hagar returning / to her adopted home

she would not have named him / nor owned
the warmth of his body

but would have left him / in the cold

of the desert / before God and the night-sky

Mary is metaphor / Symbiotic with creation / destruction
and redemption nurturing it into full fruition / Without
her God's plans are impossible / Her biological ability
to bear Christ into the world is pivotal

Her whole being is glorified in the moment because / unlike
Early Church Fathers / we now understand

that she is the human half of Christ / Her autophagy

is blessed /

Like gender / motherhood can be rethought

beyond burden and joy

As Wednesday's child is full of woe

Intertitle

IN THE AFTERGLOW OF CREATION

Veronica seeks other faces

About two weeks ago my mother / Veronica's grandmother
started shouting at the women with placards / holding their protest
in the street outside the walk-in centre where she works / Her voice
strained / grieved / my mother calls 'Ishmael? Ishmael?'

Righteous invocation is her maternal gift / We are the saints
of blasphemy / we bring nothing but heresy
in our womanly forms

My father silent in the backseat / His mouth taped
hog-tied / His daughters bring forth
nothing but trouble in this world / his consent
is his end-of-days / an eschatology of masculinity

robust / now waning

Here and now, I would like to see Mary
become the figure head

of a gender-neutral mystic sex cult'

– my Grandmother at Sunday lunch
after the death of my Grandfather

'The story has constantly to be preserved from heresy,
to be kept forcibly in the patriarchal tradition
of Christian civilisation, to be kept from too much attention
to the economies of mimicry
and the calamities of suffering.' – Donna Haraway

A group of young women make their way
to the Cathedral of Christ the Saviour / One of them
is wearing her grandmother's hat / They're there
to protest corruption in the church / They're there
to say that the belt of the Virgin / mother of God
is for all to see / not just the few that pay

Two of them are imprisoned

'Mary, your belt should bring us hope
Now it's used as rope' – Moddi's 'Punk Prayer'

Heresy must be avoided to preserve
the patriarchy / The patriarchy is
what supports the Christian institution

but exclusion / non-conformity
is what makes Christian martyrs
the practitioners of pure theatre

Or mystical experience

In the end / I resent any blind between me
and experience / Everything I touch
since the fall is heresy / I intend to touch the divine
like Mary / Julian / Margaret / Hildegard
Simone / Maria / Mother
Somewhere in between heresy and divinity
there exists something human caught
in the gleam

of the cats-eye selfie / A partial view
of the future

how little I knew / You gave
me these end of days / As an embrace

A Confusion of Marys

ANNUNCIATION MANIFESTO

(Rose M. Barron's 'Madonna Tableaux')

'We cannot live in a world that is interpreted for us
by others. An interpreted world is not a home.'
     – Hildegard von Bingen, *Selected Writings*

Outside boundaries of faith and spirituality,
the process of performing is important.
I am interested in symbols of excess,
the handcrafted construction of sets,
superficial and cultural constructs,
unexpected moments, imperfection
and humanness juxtaposed with
religious and sacred iconography.
I am re-inventing and reclaiming,
examining my identity as a woman
and twisting expectations of
what a woman represents.

ABRACADABRA

For my next trick, my lovely assistant
– give us a twirl (applause) – will
hold her book and stare into space.
I will levitate on a cloud of dry ice
– look, no wires (more applause) –
and in a moment you will see a dove
appear in a beam of light. No, there
are no secret pockets in my robes,
no mirrors or invisible strings. And,
as if by magic, she's pregnant too,
Mary, stand up and take a bow.
(Loud applause and final curtain.)

ANTARCTIC ANNUNCIATION

Stormy mix of disorganised sound,
cold air blown from the pole.
Icy improvisation melts the heart
of Mary, who would like to be
warm again, held again, home again.

It is all blue and white wind,
with angels shrieking her name
and penguins brooding. She
wonders at the strange music
of extremes, and shivers aloud.

CUT-UP ANNUNCIATION

Mystery is essential,
extremes are essential.

Spirit into matter:
the paradox resolved,

state of grace
the form of the contract,

the distance from faith
a seed of hope planted.

Some of the loveliest paintings
are meditations on absence.

FANCY DRESS ANNUNCIATION

'And what have you come as?'
'An angel.' (He's dressed in boots
and tutu, kids' wings strung
behind him.) 'Like it?' 'Nah,
not really. You shoulda shaved,
found something that fits. You
look like Tinkerbell.' (His friend
is dressed as a plain schoolgirl,
dull grey skirt and fitted blouse,
hair scraped back, red lipstick on.
They're in the kitchen at a party,
both bursting to share secrets,
gossip, find out what's going on.
Both need to have another drink.)

DAMAGED GODS

An easy typing mistake to make,
but in the context of these poems
one pertinent to belief and doubt.
Can we damage, have we damaged,

the god we wanted to believe in?
Saying the wrong thing, questioning,
ignoring, or just getting it wrong:
ambition and money, big buildings,

bad songs, an excuse for wars and
imposing our way of life on others.
Perhaps we need more words
for sorrow and despair, perhaps

we should learn how to pray again,
how to live and how to behave,
tie ourselves up in knots of thought
and accept we are just illusion.

WHAT HAVE I DONE?

'I am either owning up to myself as the cause
of such an action, qualifying my causative contribution,
or defending myself against the attribution, perhaps
locating the cause elsewhere.'
        —Judith Butler, *Giving an Account of Oneself*

A curious way of tidily containing…
kind of well shaped yet loose, unfinished.
Was it the story you were expecting?

What is Mary's role in the scheme of things?
We can know ourselves only incompletely,
can never fully choose or understand.

Perhaps we fashion our world view
according to key players we come across
or find. One could certainly look.

The madonna drawn over the bride
drawn over the matador next to the horse
drawn on the poster pasted on the wall:

layers of meaning and memory,
eyes everywhere, looking through.
It's hard to believe for long.

You walk past, disregarding stone looks
and troubled apparitions, choosing
instead your own version of events,

unwilling to take the blame
or accept yourself as damaged goods,
each moment like the first.

SHADOW ANNUNCIATION

Stick figure
in the shadow,
an angel
fallen from grace,

descended from
a cathedral world
into human space.

A cloud of doubt
and apprehension
blocks the light,

his face
his soul
his wings
burnt black as night.

FINE ART AMERICA

It's fine art America, it's city life,
Joseph's on the rooftop
dancing with his wife-to-be.
Among the water towers
and ventilation shafts,
birds come in to land,
tell them that this god
has other things planned
for them than marriage
or living in sin. Mary's
got a baby boy growing
within, like it or not.
It may be the 21st century
but this is all we've got
to hope for, hang on to,
look forward to, believe.
Joseph's getting angry
as the angel starts to leave.
It's everyday America, it's city life.
Joseph's on the rooftop
shouting at his pregnant wife.

FORGOTTEN ANNUNCIATION

It's not there unless you squint
and pull a face. It's clearer
later in the day when the sun
is not as bright and comes
from a different direction.

The smudge of white's an angel,
the cream mark is Mary, who has
abandoned the confined spaces
which were once blue behind her.
My memory's faint and faded too.

PIXELATED ANNUNCIATION

low res freeze frame
digital slippage

jagged silhouettes
squares of grey

sharp-edged clouds
dark lines of light

Mary a blur of tones
old software glitch

angel all jitter
and awkwardness

this annunciation's
low res freeze frame

IN NAME ONLY

This one's reduced to simple shapes:
rows of arches, curves of body,
wings swept back, round discs
for heads. Is it a sketch to work out
composition, or an impersonal version
which can stand for everyone or nobody,
an annunciation in name only?

KEEPING IT IN PERSPECTIVE

Art criticism conjectures the snail in Francesco del Cossa's *Annunciation* as a visual balance but also as indicative of 15th Century self-awareness, the flatness of the scene, the knowledge that Nazareth was not at all like this.

Mary cannot even see the angel, her view is blocked by the pillar which symbolises God in the room. The city beyond, painted in detailed perspective, could not be built, but looks impressive.

Architects and planners are discussing new ways to create multigenerational living, or at least offer the possibility to those who may not desire it or perhaps know what an extended family is.

There is no end to the progress of knowledge and science, although funding is hard to come by. Every research meeting I go to interests me and I theoretically relocate my work. But I have been to too many meetings, changed my ideas too many times.

We keep coming back to the fact that arts improve the quality of life although that cannot be substantiated or statistically proven, and I do not want my poetry to work through empathy or ego.

There is no end to the ways this story can be told.

GAME PLAN

It's like chess. Angel to queen:
check mate. The king has decided,
the game is won. It's black and white,
clear cut. But who is playing who?

HARVEST

A sisterly angel
confides in Mary,
sharing a secret
she doesn't want
to know, the dove
simply sits in a tree.
The angel's friendly
and approachable,
not scary at all;
both women wear
simple frocks
and go barefoot.
Perhaps the angel
will help with
the apple picking?
Everything's
ripe for plucking.

A CONFUSION OF MARYS

'With your long blonde hair and your eyes of blue
The only thing I ever got from you
Was sorrow, sorrow'
  —David Bowie, 'Sorrow'

as if

a true portrait

sorrows known   sorrows shared

solitude

swords in shoulders

seven sorrows

seven moments of despair

venerated images

statues carried everywhere

a madonna in the window

graffiti on the wall

neon halo in the twilight

shadows in the square

a confusion of stories   ideas and myth

    stone tears   moving eyes

      as if   as if

    everyone else is a non-believer

WHAT THE ANGELS SING TO THEMSELVES

We're always making plans for ~~Nigel~~ Mary
We only want what's best for ~~him~~ her
We're only making plans for ~~Nigel~~ Mary
~~Nigel~~ Mary just needs this helping hand

KINDRED SPIRITS
after Chiharu Shiota

To be filled with time, to be filled with time, an empty canvas made from white dreams, her bed warm with spider love and silence, desire and song. A wedding will not take place but the empty past is there for all to see. Tomorrow pours through a slot in time, ready to fill the future, festooned in desire. Her bed is extra large, warm with silence and love; ash hangs in charcoal music. Sleep tight. My nightmare is an abandoned stage: angel long gone, adrift in a boat, Mary's silhouette outlined and full of dreams. My room is filled with breath, pouring down the wall, ready to run away after we have packed small bags and planned our escape. I am knotted tight in the corner, waiting to be filled with air among the shadows, where images pile up. Webs of meaning and association, hidden steps and messages we cannot read, linear shadows and sleeping souls; kindred spirits in a place we are not allowed to visit.

META-ANNUNCIATION

'My icon status is that of the mother. Artemis and many others precede me, no doubt back to the stone age. The difference with me is passivity and sorrow.'
—Mary the Mother of God, *Art Review*

The art critic invents a voice for Mary the Mother of God and interrogates her about contemporary art and her role in the grand scheme of things. A friend of mine is more concerned that the *why* is missing, that the annunciation is simply a given and that our protagonist is caught up in something there is no reason for.

Perhaps she doesn't know either, but doubt, confusion, incredulity are not enough. What is God's motive? Does he have a convincing rationale? Do the angels never question? Perhaps asking questions of ourselves is enough?

Do not forget that these are poems about paintings, not a philosophical or theological debate.

THE MOST VISIBLE WOMAN IN HISTORY

Models of appropriate female behaviour, doomed to fall short of their goals, madonnas are often glitzed up and a bit sexy, but all have human needs and wants.

Focus on sensuality and postponing parenthood, excluding women from the inevitable phenomena of nature, in order to represent the variety of ways women live today, confronting the conflicting roles they are expected to play.

CAMPSITE ANNUNCIATION

Mary's living in a bunk house in the woods, open to the elements, hung with flowers and lights. She's a good girl, puts her shoes in the corner, prays each night, is not surprised when an angel wrapped in a red blanket leans through the window and offers her a lily. Light streams around, from and through him. She is suddenly scared and shy, knows summer is at an end. She kneels beside her bed and tries out the words 'mother', 'god' and 'son'. Feels the small, square rug beneath her knees, then packs her things and goes to look for Joseph. He'll know what to do.

ANGELS AND OTHER STRANGERS

Angels are too good to be true, the devil has all the best tunes, although you are more likely to meet a stranger than an angel.

Someone spoke of divine interventions, of redemption, but we are beyond saving. These days there are not many stories left that I have confidence in.

I can tell I am not greatly interested any more, may be speaking just so I can speak: phonetics meet semantics.

Open your mouth and words come out.

THE LAST THING SHE NEEDS

She over-carefully
folds the clean washing,
studiously ignoring
whatever is behind her
and what it is trying
to say. Life must go on,
she thinks, as normal.

There is so much to do.
The last thing she needs
is angels or annunciations,
more bother or surprises.
It gently waits, insistent,
until she is ready to listen,
prepared to hear. It can

wait for ever, has waited
half an eternity to come
and find this woman.
The stars are aligned,
the earth awaits,
this housewife puts
housework aside.

LEVITATING ANNUNCIATION

He catches a thermal,
glides across the room,
pink suit perfectly crumpled.

She's used to showoffs,
hardly moves a muscle
or raises an eyebrow.

They're both busy
being cool, waiting
to see who'll speak first,

if the smoking volcano
in the distance will erupt
in flame or gently subside.

THREE SCREENS IN A DARKENED ROOM

The Annunciation, Marian Ilmestys

The future is about to happen live. It is
hard to take it all in at once, harder to
make sense of any of it. Donkey does
as donkeys do, caged birds make noise
as we pan from dovecot to church tower
where time hangs in an empty space
and a bell-ringer appears to control
a flying woman whose face is hidden
until a trapeze comes into view as
the camera pulls ever so slowly back.

Architectural plans of the cathedral
keep things in perspective and suggest
a possible vanishing point, a way out
of the conundrum, which is yet to be
explained. But here comes the angel,
this time a crow-like figure hanging
through a makeshift window. Mary
shies away from the holy apparition
in altarpieces elsewhere, but here
it's more a chance to have a gossip,

whilst her friends listen in.
It's cold outside and the wind
whistles through portico and arches
which are mystically aligned. A sign!
Chairs reassemble themselves
in mismatched groups as Mary
shadows herself onscreen. Everything
is left unsaid and God soon flies off,
leaving the house cleaned and tidied,
screens fading as the audience disperses.

ANGELIC DEPARTURE

'Even on impossible journeys, we are not alone.'
　—David Rothenberg, *Sudden Music*

The angels are leaving, taking a boat across the water, perhaps to find a country where people still believe.

One has already lost his wings, because they said he was an impossible idea, a religious metaphor for messages from heaven.

Neither angels nor heaven exist, of course. Watch the empty boat drift away from shore.

AFTERWARDS

When the dust settles, and her heart's
stopped racing, when she can see again,
after being dazzled, when what was said
has finally sunk in, Mary screams,
shouts at the world for being unfair,
and collapses angrily into a chair.

How dare a god interfere like this?
How dare he impregnate her!
Her betrothal is now worthless,
no-one will believe what happened,
Joseph will never speak to her again
and everyone will talk about her.

She's never believed in angels
but can't deny he was here or what
he said. She hopes the neighbours
weren't listening, hopes if she shuts
her eyes for a while, the whole thing
will have turned into a dream.

But she knows that's the worst way
to end a story, to undo the reader's
investment, knows it's not going
to happen, nothing can be changed.
Motherhood, virginity and sainthood
are the crosses she will have to bear.

NOTES

In addition to many internet images and sites, I would like to specifically acknowledge the following source material. The list is by no means complete.

Eija-Liisa Ahtila (K21/Hatje Cantz)
Take A Closer Look, Daniel Arasse
Known and Strange Things, Teju Cole
'Great Critics and Their Ideas No 55: Mary the Mother of God on LD50 and
    Damien Hirst', interview by Matthew Collings in *Art Review*
'A Slightly Less Creepy Annunciation', Tom Johnson, in *The Tangential*
The Annunciation, Lino Mannocci
Picabia 1879-1953, (Scottish National Gallery of Modern Art)
The Hand Lines, Chiharu Shiota
Annunciation (Phaidon)

I would like to apologise to XTC, and to thank Clark Allison, Mike Ferguson and Sarah Law for their comments on and interest in this project, Martin Caseley for help with ordering the book, and Sarah Cave for writing part of it.

RML

Thank you to Luke, Celia, Rupert, Luke K, & my family for their unfailing creative support.

SC

MONOCHROME GIRL

for Sarah

No grey or charcoal blue
would do, she only wanted
Ad Reinhardt's black holes
that removed the light
from bright galleries
and took language away,
left her speechless,
looking at the wall;
or Ryman's white on white,
a purer form of absence,
a dead mirror, a primed
experience waiting to happen.
John Cage made her listen,
Agnes Martin mesmerized
with pale stripes, but they
were too noisy and colourful
for a monochrome girl living
in a world of shadow and sun
where hermits wrote poems,
each on their own island;
sent them to her in dreams.

COLOURFUL BOY

Adrift in a spectrum of noise,
lost and confused in colour,
he aims for pattern and order,
navigates by chaos and chance.
He wants Peter Lanyon's blues,
the glide path of his brush;
Hoyland's stains and trowelled-
on diagonal divides, the buzz
and static of contrasting tones.
Sean Scully's stripes are form
enough for him, the wax grid
of Andrew Bick a safety net
to fall into as Diebenkorn's
Ocean Park series serenade.
He is shouting out in delight,
channelling reflected rainbows
in the possibilities of paint.

www.ingramcontent.com/pod-product-compliance
Lightning Source LLC
Chambersburg PA
CBHW031933080426
42734CB00007B/668